leaving and going across the street, my mom went on the inside and said, "All right, you guys walk on the outside. Men always protect the ladies from the traffic." My brothers and I started to march to the beat of the drum, obedient to what my mom said because we respected and loved her.

Once we got to the mall, we went inside the double doors, but my mom stayed outside the doors and just waited in front of them. My brothers and I looked at each other, dumbfounded and baffled by my mom not automatically walking in the door. So we walked outside the door, and my mom said to us, "Men always open the door for women," and we said, "Yes ma'am, let me open the door with pleasure." That lesson was baked into me from that day on. If that is not an example of what prior knowledge looks like, I don't know what else I can tell you. She baked that into me, which became an expectation for me.

When my wife and I first started dating, this is something I did often. She never walked on the outside of the street, and she never opened the door. She wasn't used to someone doing it consistently because some guys can play a game with that to seem like a gentleman to get closer to their goal of what they want from a woman. I get that. Little did she know that was literally baked into me since I was a kid, so no, there was not a game being played by these actions.

II. Observation: Family and social observations also shape expectations. That is, our family has done things that we see them do, such as how they manage money, talk about love, resolve conflicts, communicate, and so on. Observing people we care about and respect from a young age teaches us what to expect in different situations, and our natural programming acts out what we see. This is also true of our observations of society as children.

When I was younger, my mom had the responsibility of raising five boys by herself. When I reflect back, I always tell people that my mom was both a brick and a teddy bear. Even under tough circumstances, she showed warmth, laughter, and affection towards my brothers and me. As a result, I still carry the expectation that people should be warm and affectionate with each other.

When I meet people, I'm not one for handshakes - I'm a hugger. I believe I give the best hugs because my mom taught my brothers and me that showing affection through physical touch is okay. I understand that not everyone has come from a background like mine, but I still carry this expectation to this day.

Overall, my mom's example has taught me the importance of showing warmth and affection towards others, even under tough circumstances. While I understand that not everyone may be comfortable with physical touch, I'm willing to respect people's boundaries and find other ways to show my appreciation and affection towards them.

Let's talk about the third way expectations are formed.

III. Personal Experience: Expectations are shaped by personal experiences. You will encounter situations in life that will shape your expectations about certain things in order to protect yourself from being hurt again. Whether the pain is physical or mental, you set an expectation for yourself to protect yourself from your own life experiences.

When I was about 11 years old, my mom didn't come home from work at her usual time. At the time, my mom and stepdad were dating, and my stepdad came over to cook dinner for my brothers and me and make sure we were okay. We had a house phone at the time, and my dad received a call that my mom had been in a pretty bad car accident with a co-worker who was like an aunt figure to us.

The accident was caused by someone who had stolen a car and ran a stop sign, hitting my mom and the aunt. My mom's airbag didn't work, and she was slammed against the dashboard, causing damage to her chest. The next day, my mom returned home from the hospital in a taxi with a small plastic bin to spit up blood from internal bleeding. Her chest was riddled with black, dark blue, and purple bruises, and I never forgot seeing her in that much pain and discomfort.

My mom never had a driver's license, even though she's from Jersey City, where you don't have to drive. One reason could be that she never learned how to drive or didn't care for it, but the real reason is her experience in that car accident. Even though she's been driving around with my stepdad for the past 23 years, I can still hear her voice in my head saying, "Slow down, Ben. Watch where you're going, Ben." It's not because my stepdad doesn't know how to drive, but because of the personal experience that caused her trauma and still gives her anxiety to this day when she's in a car.

When we give birth to these expectations from these three different areas, we begin to see things in a different light. We still carry these expectations with us to this day if we haven't gone through the process of re-engineering and inspecting these expectations. We usually avoid people who do not agree with our expectations so that we do not have to stretch our understanding and grow. Then we find ourselves repeating the same experiences, but only because we never investigated our experiences or the expectations that underlies them. You'll be able to trace it back to something you noticed if you look back.

Let's move on to the second stage of the Expectation Journey so that we can further understand where you are in your inner conversation.

2. Perception

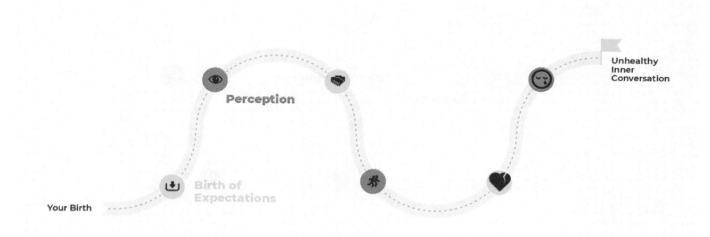

You see the world through the lens of your expectations when you have full-blown expectations in place at this point in your life. I'd like to refer to your perception as the vision of your expectations. Why am I saying this? Your perception is how you see the world based on the expectations you form as a result of your experiences and knowledge.

Your perception is now extremely powerful. Your perception is so strong that it determines where you go, what you do, and why you do it. Your way of thinking makes you think about opportunities in terms of whether they will help you or hurt you. Your perception matches your expectations, and it causes you to perceive people as positive or negative.

When this perception is in place, you proceed to the third stage of the expectation journey.

Stage 3: Commitment

3. Commitment

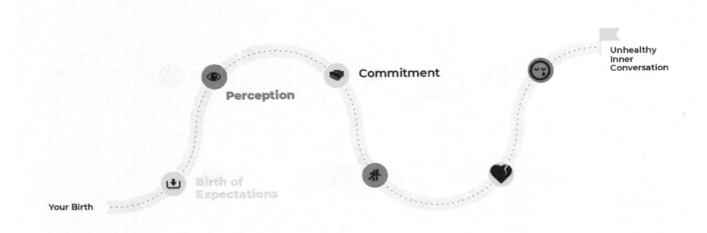

People who say they want to do something but don't have any expectations about it are one of my pet peeves. Don't be fooled; everyone commits to something with the expectation of gaining something from it. We never put ourselves in situations where we know we will lose something on purpose. We put ourselves in situations that promise us something beneficial in exchange for our actions to obtain it. This is why we make promises and commitments as significant as a college major, a job, a relationship, or a date. Small commitments, such as the clothes we wear, jewelry we wear, and food we eat. Everything we commit to and engage in has a backend benefit that we have been taught will provide us with. As previously stated, our perception is the vision of our expectation. When you commit to something, you're not committing to doing nothing in order to get something; you're committing to taking action in order to achieve a specific result, which brings us to stage 4 of the expectation journey.

Stage 4: Action

4. Action

In life, we take action for a variety of reasons. Whether you express it or not, you're acting with the intention of gaining something that will make you feel good. Making you feel good for that moment or something that can make you feel good in the long run even if the temporary action is not as pleasing. The actions we take are based on the commitments we make, whether small or large, and the commitments we make are based on our perception of the benefit we will receive from this thing. The perception we have of the world around us is based on the expectations we have in place to protect ourselves so that we only gain and do not suffer. With all of that said, what happens when the promises made by our actions are not kept? To put it another way, what happens when the expectation that drove our perception, commitment and now action is unmet?

Let's talk about it in Stage 5 of the Expectations Journey.

5. Unmet Expectations

Okay, I think we're getting somewhere, but buckle up because things are about to get serious. You had an expectation, a perception of something, you committed to it, you took action, and you expected a promise to meet that expectation inside of you on the back end. You've hit a roadblock in your desire to have your expectations met. Your expectations have not been met. And, listen, I can't fault you for all of your efforts and the thought you put into this opportunity before committing to it, and now you're in this position where you have unmet expectations in whatever situation you're in. unmet expectations at work, in relationships, in business, in family, in your physical appearance by the summer, and so on. Unmet expectations produce feelings within us that we do not want.

Let's talk about what happens when your expectations aren't met, as well as Stage 6 of the Expectation Journey.

6. Dealing With Unmet Expectations

The feelings you will experience from an unmet expectation will usually follow the prefix "un." You know what I mean; let's talk about it for a second. Undesirable, unpleasant, uncomfortable—do these emotions ring a bell to you? These are some of the emotions you will encounter on your journey of unmet expectations. What usually happens when you have unmet expectations?

There are two things people usually do when they have unmet expectations that produce undesirable, unpleasant, and uncomfortable feelings in the situation.

1. Unhealthy Coping: When people are confronted with negative emotions, the first thing they do is seek coping mechanisms. Now, coping mechanisms are not inherently bad, so let me rephrase that to say that when confronted with uncomfortable feelings, people will resort to unhealthy coping mechanisms, which are usually the first option. Why is this the case? simply because coping is easier than any of the other options available to people when an expectation is not met. Excessive complaining, excessive use of social media, overeating, emotional eating, pornography, finding someone to have sex with, searching for love and relationships to make you feel good, alcohol and drug addiction, and even therapy are all forms of coping. Yes, I did say therapy. Some people will use a good thing like therapy as a coping mechanism simply to talk out their feelings, believing that once they have done so, everything will be fine, but they will leave their sessions feeling the same way they did before

the session. Humans are wired to want to feel good in order to achieve emotional or spiritual balance. This is natural; I understand. There is, however, a distinction between coping and soothing yourself to feel better. That's a different topic for another book. All of this is to say that when we have unmet expectations, this is the first place we look. We want to cope and avoid the negative feelings of disappointment.

The problem is that even though you started using unhealthy coping mechanisms as a result of an unmet expectation, the expectation you had for yourself did not go away. As a result, whenever you think about the expectation not being met, you will continue to cope and abandon the expectation that you had just to feel good.

2. Toxic Positivity/Spirituality: The second thing people will do if their expectations are not met is something that society encourages people to do when they face disappointment or setbacks. Society wants you to be strong, keep going, push forward, and have a positive attitude. While I agree with having a perseverance mindset and going after what you want despite disappointment, I disagree with how we've been conditioned to do it. I can speak from personal experience. Coming from a poverty-stricken environment, being homeless several times, and being financially down on my luck—the list of everything I've been through is endless. I've been recognized for my positive attitude and ability to get out of a bad situation in order to improve my situation and get my finances in order. But no one ever asked me, "How are you?" rather than, "What are you doing?" It is critical that we do not engage in "toxic positivity." What exactly do I mean by "toxic positivity"? Toxic positivity encompasses a wide range of activities that people can engage in to maintain a positive mindset and continue to pursue a goal after experiencing a deeply disappointing or unpleasant feeling. Consuming motivational books, reciting motivational chants, being grateful, meditating, and even offering praise and worship to the God you believe in exclusively are examples of these things. Now, I'm not saying you shouldn't pray to or praise the God you worship when you're going through a difficult time or feeling bad. God, in my opinion, meets you right where you are. He wants you to make it through and experience everything he has in store for you. I believe that God wants you to pray when you are experiencing negative feelings and emotions. I don't think that's where He wants you to stop. I believe that God meets us where we are and leads us through a process about our feelings and emotions so that we do not engage in toxic positivity or toxic spirituality to achieve a specific goal or meet a specific expectation. When this happens, our expectations take precedence over God himself.

The truth is that we may eventually reach our goals or expectations if we practice toxic positivity or spirituality. The issue is, how will you get to your expectation or goal? More than likely, you'll arrive emotionally bruised, soulless, and disconnected from your true self. Why is this the case? Because you went through the process of meeting this expectation of yourself by stuffing down your true feelings and quoting scriptures, praying and praising, meditating and being grateful, and chanting motivational mantras, you left no time to be honest with yourself about how you truly felt when that expectation was not met.

I understand. I understand why you might not want to slow down and check in on yourself, and there could be several reasons for this.

Reason 1: Perhaps you were never taught how to check in with yourself emotionally. You were probably taught that checking in on yourself emotionally is for weaklings and that you must power through it.

Reason 2: You may believe that if you process your emotions right now, you will give up or crack because you don't know how to do it in a way that will allow you to come out on the other side with healthy emotions and accomplish your goal or expectation.

I recall having a particularly difficult year and refusing to cry. I didn't want to cry because I was afraid of what was beyond that. I was homeless, about to lose my car, and had just given birth to my first child. I was going on job interviews, showering in gyms before an interview, and getting ready in locker rooms. I remember feeling strong emotions that I couldn't put into words. I had no idea what words to use to express those emotions because I had never been taught to provide them with all the words they required. So instead of breaking down or crying, I turned to positive mantras, quotes, and willpower when I wanted to cry or show how I felt. The truth is that I "leveled up." I got a good job.

I'm glad I was able to get that job and eventually get a new car because the one I was worried about losing was repossessed. I was sitting in my new house, a nice townhouse, with my Mercedes-Benz outside, doing a great job leading and training people, but when I got home, it was difficult to face the silence. It was difficult to face myself because I arrived at my destination with pieces of my soul missing. So, what exactly did I do? I began doing the two things I'm about to mention. I started to deal with things in unhealthy ways, and I also used willpower as a way to avoid dealing with my unmet expectations that I had met along the way but never dealt with. I realized I needed to process what was going on inside of me. At the time, I deleted my social media accounts and began to seek peace of mind in the midst of the internal chaos I didn't know what to do with.

That year, I began going to therapy, and it changed my life. It changed my life because it taught me how to recognize what was going on inside of me, how to properly process my emotions, and how to practice the habit of healing even when I wasn't in therapy sessions. I had a fantastic therapist, but I can't give him all the credit. I was eager to learn and grow. With all of my years of experience as a natural-born trainer, facilitator, and coach, it was easy for me to see patterns in what was going on inside of me as I went through therapy. As I saw the patterns of what was going on, I was able to document my personal journey and put it into a system that helped me develop the habit of healing daily, and I created a process that helps me grow every day in every area of my life.

As I began to heal, every aspect of my life began to change: my purpose changed, my expectations changed, and, as previously stated, my goals changed as the true me began to emerge.

Okay, I went off on a tangent, but I believe it was beneficial. Let's get back to work. I mentioned three approaches to dealing with unmet expectations. The third response to unmet expectations is exactly what I was referring to earlier. Let's find out what it is.

What's the best way to handle the feelings of unmet expectations?

Healthily Processing Your Undesirable Emotions

As a third way to deal with unmet and unhealthy expectations, people can healthily process unhealthy and unpleasant feelings. If you use this method to deal with your negative feelings when an expectation isn't met, you will have renewed faith, healthy action steps, and maybe even a new expectation in place of the old one once you figure out where the old expectation came from and how it led you to have an unhealthy conversation with yourself.

Gentlemen and ladies, While you're reading this book, I'd like to introduce you to a process that I've developed that many clients have used to change their lives at any given point by experiencing healthy emotions when confronted with unmet expectations and eventually achieving healthy expectations that they set in place.

This is known as the 4A Process. This process will help you navigate your unhealthy inner conversation that is born from your expectations, as well as re-engineer your unhealthy conversation and create a healthy conversation with yourself so that you can have healthy relationships with everyone else.

Let's see how much you remember from what we just learned. Here are some questions for you to answer:

1. What are expectations?
   a) Something that you strongly believe will happen in the future.
   b) Something that you strongly believe won't happen in the future.
   c) Something that might happen in the future.

2. What are the characteristics of expectations?
   a) They are often unspoken and can be your own internal voice of right and wrong.
   b) They are always spoken and can be someone else's external voice of right and wrong.
   c) They have no characteristics.

3. Are expectations bad?
   a) Yes.
   b) No.
   c) It depends on the situation.

4. When do unhealthy conversations begin?
   a) Stage 1: The Birth of Expectations.
   b) Stage 2: Perception.
   c) Stage 5: Unmet Expectations.

5. What is perception?
   a) Seeing the world through your own expectations.
   b) Seeing the world through someone else's expectations.
   c) Seeing the world without any expectations.

6. What is stage 3 of the expectation journey?
   a) Perception.
   b) Action.
   c) Commitment.

7. What is toxic positivity/spirituality?
   a) Dismissing or invalidating emotions.
   b) Focusing only on positive aspects of a situation.
   c) Both a and b.

8. What are the reasons for toxic positivity/spirituality?
   a) Not being taught to check in with your emotions.
   b) Being afraid of giving up or breaking down while processing emotions.
   c) Both a and b.

And that's it! How did you do?

Answer Key:

1. Answer: a) Something that you strongly believe will happen in the future.
2. Answer: a) They are often unspoken and can be your own internal voice of right and wrong.
3. Answer: c) It depends on the situation.
4. Answer: c) Stage 5: Unmet Expectations.
5. Answer: a) Seeing the world through your own expectations.
6. Answer: c) Commitment.
7. Answer: c) Both a and b.
8. Answer: c) Both a and b.

Let's get started with the 4A Process!

The 4A Process

Okay, you've been hearing me talk about this 4A process, which has led to so much growth in myself and my clients.

What is the 4A Process?

The 4A Process is a set of questions and prompts designed to help you reflect and go deep within yourself.

The 4A Process consists of four words that begin with the letter A.

The four steps in the 4A process include:

1. Awareness: Having the ability to identify your feelings is imperative to self-growth.
2. Address it: Get to the root of the feelings you've identified.
3. Accept it: Having reached this point of reflection, it's time to come to terms with the reality of your situation.
4. Accelerate: It's time to move forward with healthy action steps that lead to long-lasting growth and joy.

In this workbook, we're going to use the 4A Process to have a healthier conversation with yourself that will result in creating and maintaining healthy relationships.

The goal of this 4A Process is to help you find and talk about the unhealthy, unspoken expectations you have in different parts of your life that led to these feelings and are making it hard for you to have healthy relationships. When I say healthy relationships, I mean anything from friendship and family to a romantic interest to professional relationships.

Remember, all unpleasant and undesirable feelings come from unmet expectations. The goal of this 4A Process is to help you put words to the unspoken unhealthy conversation you had along your expectation journey that made you feel bad and led you to either cope in an unhealthy way or use willpower (aka toxic positivity) to reach your expectation.

Let's get started with going through the 4A Process.

We'll begin with the first "A": Awareness.

Awareness

Sparking Awareness & Labeling Your Feelings

In 2013, when I was living in Brooklyn, one of my mentors, Terry Winston, looked around the room in a meeting where he had asked a question. The question was, "What is the best teacher in life?" Everyone in the room answers pretty similarly by answering "experience." He emphatically said "no" and paused for a second. He said that "evaluated experience" is the best teacher in life.

When he said this, it made me freeze and think for a second. I thought to myself, "I've never heard this before." Even though he said those words to me in 2013, they didn't make sense until 2020, when I began to process what was going on inside of me. The first step to processing the unhealthy conversations you're having with yourself that were born from your expectations is becoming aware of what you are feeling when those expectations go unmet.

The questions I'm about to ask you will guide you into answering them or help you become aware of exactly what's going on in a particular area of your life, and they will also help you put into words what you are feeling from those unmet expectations that have you feeling the way you are.

Let's get started by assessing the different areas of your life to spark awareness.

The 4A Assessment

The 4A Assessment is designed to help you identify and address the areas of your life that need the most attention. This process will not work if you are not completely honest with yourself concerning what's going on in the following areas of your life.

Rate your level of satisfaction on a scale of 1 to 5, with 1 being 'Very Dissatisfied' and 5 being 'Very Satisfied'. Circle the number that matches your level of satisfaction.)

Circle your choice

1. Health & Wellness

Physical, Mental & Spiritual Health

How satisfied are you with your physical health?

This includes your food choices, elimination, rest/sleep, hydration (water intake), exercise/ flexibility & self care

Satisfaction Levels	Very Dissatisfied	Somewhat Dissatisfied	Neutral	Somewhat Satisfied	Very Satisfied
Satisfaction Rating	1	2	3	4	5

How satisfied are you with your current mental health?

This includes your stress management, ability to find healthy coping activities, managing anxiety, therapy sessions, reading books, taking courses etc.

Satisfaction Levels	Very Dissatisfied	Somewhat Dissatisfied	Neutral	Somewhat Satisfied	Very Satisfied
Satisfaction Rating	1	2	3	4	5

How satisfied are you with your current spiritual health?

This includes your relationship with God, maybe even your prayer life, serving others, having a community of like minded individuals spiritually, sense of purpose, showing and growing in your faith

Satisfaction Levels	Very Dissatisfied	Somewhat Dissatisfied	Neutral	Somewhat Satisfied	Very Satisfied
Satisfaction Rating	1	2	3	4	5

To calculate your overall rating for this area, please add up your satisfaction ratings for each of the three categories (physical health, mental health, and spiritual health) and divide by three.

Satisfaction levels:

1. Very Dissatisfied: Extremely unhappy with the area of your health and wellness
2. Somewhat Dissatisfied: Moderately unhappy with the area of your health and wellness
3. Neutral: Neither happy nor unhappy with the area of your health and wellness
4. Somewhat Satisfied: Moderately happy with the area of your health and wellness
5. Very Satisfied: Extremely happy with the area of your health and wellness

Overall rating for Health & Wellness: _____ / 5

2. Life Fulfillment

Creative & Recreational Fulfillment

How satisfied are you with your current creative abilities?

This includes your utilizing your gifts & talents, setting worthwhile goals, planning & brainstorming ideas, doing purpose work

Satisfaction Levels	Very Dissatisfied	Somewhat Dissatisfied	Neutral	Somewhat Satisfied	Very Satisfied
Satisfaction Rating	1	2	3	4	5

How satisfied are you with the way you use your leisure time right now?

This includes your enjoying your favorite hobbies, entertainment, travel/vacations & decompressing intentionally?

Satisfaction Levels	Very Dissatisfied	Somewhat Dissatisfied	Neutral	Somewhat Satisfied	Very Satisfied
Satisfaction Rating	1	2	3	4	5

To calculate your overall rating for this area, please add up your satisfaction ratings for each of the two categories (creative abilities and recreational fulfillment) and divide by two.

Satisfaction levels:

1. Very Dissatisfied: Extremely unhappy with the area of your life fulfillment
2. Somewhat Dissatisfied: Moderately unhappy with the area of your life fulfillment
3. Neutral: Neither happy nor unhappy with the area of your life fulfillment
4. Somewhat Satisfied: Moderately happy with the area of your life fulfillment
5. Very Satisfied: Extremely happy with the area of your life fulfillment

Overall rating for Life Fulfillment: _____ / 5

3. Relationships

Friendships, Romantic, Family & Professional

How satisfied are you with your relationships with your family?
This includes your level of conversation, feelings of connectedness, and desire for stronger relationships.

Satisfaction Levels	Very Dissatisfied	Somewhat Dissatisfied	Neutral	Somewhat Satisfied	Very Satisfied
Satisfaction Rating	1	2	3	4	5

How satisfied are you with your current love life?

This includes your dating life, current relationship, or marriage. Are you getting what you desire? Are there any unprocessed feelings about something that has happened or is happening? Is there a conversation that needs to be had?

Satisfaction Levels	Very Dissatisfied	Somewhat Dissatisfied	Neutral	Somewhat Satisfied	Very Satisfied
Satisfaction Rating	1	2	3	4	5

How satisfied are you with your friendships?

This includes your desire to have better friends, unspoken things that need to be spoken of, or your desire to be a better friend.

Satisfaction Levels	Very Dissatisfied	Somewhat Dissatisfied	Neutral	Somewhat Satisfied	Very Satisfied
Satisfaction Rating	1	2	3	4	5

How satisfied are you with professional relationships?

This includes your ability to work with people around you that are in alignment with your values or speaking up for yourself in a healthy way to make your work environment less stressful.

Satisfaction Levels	Very Dissatisfied	Somewhat Dissatisfied	Neutral	Somewhat Satisfied	Very Satisfied
Satisfaction Rating	1	2	3	4	5

To calculate your overall rating for the Relationships area, please add up your satisfaction ratings for each of the four categories (family, love life, friendships, and professional relationships) and divide by four.

Here's the satisfaction level scale:

1. Very Dissatisfied: Extremely unhappy with the area of your relationships
2. Somewhat Dissatisfied: Moderately unhappy with the area of your relationships
3. Neutral: Neither happy nor unhappy with the area of your relationships
4. Somewhat Satisfied: Moderately happy with the area of your relationships
5. Very Satisfied: Extremely happy with the area of your relationships

Overall rating for Relationships: _____ / 5

4. Personal Productivity

This area includes:
- **time management**
- **home upkeep**
- **transportation upkeep**

How satisfied are you with how you've been consistently managing your time?

This includes your ability to create and stick to the routines you've set to accomplish important goals and tasks.

Satisfaction Levels	Very Dissatisfied	Somewhat Dissatisfied	Neutral	Somewhat Satisfied	Very Satisfied
Satisfaction Rating	1	2	3	4	5

How satisfied are you with how you're managing the upkeep of your current living space?

This includes your ability to clean and organize your living space in a way that provides a place for peace and productivity.

Satisfaction Levels	Very Dissatisfied	Somewhat Dissatisfied	Neutral	Somewhat Satisfied	Very Satisfied
Satisfaction Rating	1	2	3	4	5

How satisfied are you with how you're maintaining the functionality and availability of your mode of transportation?

This includes your ability to proactively keep your transportation performing at its best and keeping it clean.

Satisfaction Levels	Very Dissatisfied	Somewhat Dissatisfied	Neutral	Somewhat Satisfied	Very Satisfied
Satisfaction Rating	1	2	3	4	5

To calculate your overall rating for the Personal Productivity area, please add up your satisfaction ratings for each of the three categories (time management, home upkeep, and transportation upkeep) and divide by three.

Here's the satisfaction level scale:

1. Very Dissatisfied: Extremely unhappy with the area of your personal productivity
2. Somewhat Dissatisfied: Moderately unhappy with the area of your personal productivity
3. Neutral: Neither happy nor unhappy with the area of your personal productivity
4. Somewhat Satisfied: Moderately happy with the area of your personal productivity
5. Very Satisfied: Extremely happy with the area of your personal productivity

Overall rating for Personal Productivity: _____ / 5

5. Career

This includes your job and/or business development

How satisfied are you with your current job or business status?

Satisfaction Levels	Very Dissatisfied	Somewhat Dissatisfied	Neutral	Somewhat Satisfied	Very Satisfied
Satisfaction Rating	1	2	3	4	5

How satisfied are you with your current job position or the position your business is in?

Satisfaction Levels	Very Dissatisfied	Somewhat Dissatisfied	Neutral	Somewhat Satisfied	Very Satisfied
Satisfaction Rating	1	2	3	4	5

How satisfied are you with your current work environment?

Satisfaction Levels	Very Dissatisfied	Somewhat Dissatisfied	Neutral	Somewhat Satisfied	Very Satisfied
Satisfaction Rating	1	2	3	4	5

To calculate your overall rating for the Job/Business Development area, please add up your satisfaction ratings for each of the three categories (current job or business status, job position or business position, and work environment) and divide by three.

Here's the satisfaction level scale:

1. Very Dissatisfied: Extremely unhappy with the area of your job/business development
2. Somewhat Dissatisfied: Moderately unhappy with the area of your job/business development
3. Neutral: Neither happy nor unhappy with the area of your job/business development
4. Somewhat Satisfied: Moderately happy with the area of your job/business development
5. Very Satisfied: Extremely happy with the area of your job/business development

Overall rating for Job/Business Development: _____ / 5

6. Finances

This includes your wealth building & money management

How satisfied are you with your ability to retire when you would like?

Satisfaction Levels	Very Dissatisfied	Somewhat Dissatisfied	Neutral	Somewhat Satisfied	Very Satisfied
Satisfaction Rating	1	2	3	4	5

How satisfied are you with what you will leave behind for the generations behind you financially?

Satisfaction Levels	Very Dissatisfied	Somewhat Dissatisfied	Neutral	Somewhat Satisfied	Very Satisfied
Satisfaction Rating	1	2	3	4	5

How satisfied are you with your current investments?

Satisfaction Levels	Very Dissatisfied	Somewhat Dissatisfied	Neutral	Somewhat Satisfied	Very Satisfied
Satisfaction Rating	1	2	3	4	5

How satisfied are you with your current money management?

This includes your budgeting, savings, and spending habits.

Satisfaction Levels	Very Dissatisfied	Somewhat Dissatisfied	Neutral	Somewhat Satisfied	Very Satisfied
Satisfaction Rating	1	2	3	4	5

To calculate your overall rating for the Finances area, please add up your satisfaction ratings for each of the five categories (retirement planning, generational wealth, investments, and money management) and divide by four.

Here's the satisfaction level scale:

1. Very Dissatisfied: Extremely unhappy with the area of your finances
2. Somewhat Dissatisfied: Moderately unhappy with the area of your finances
3. Neutral: Neither happy nor unhappy with the area of your finances
4. Somewhat Satisfied: Moderately happy with the area of your finances
5. Very Satisfied: Extremely happy with the area of your finances

Overall rating for Finances: _____ / 5

Alright, let's revisit the assessment and identify the area of your life that received the lowest rating. Once you've pinpointed it, we can dive deeper and bring more awareness to what's going on in that particular area. To make the most of this process, let's get specific about the particular aspect of that area of life that you want to focus on. For example, if it's related to health and wellness, decide whether you want to process your spiritual, physical, or emotional health. Once you've chosen a specific area to focus on, we can move forward to answering the following questions and specifically process any unhealthy inner conversation happening in that area.

Sounds good?

Let's take this next step together.

Awareness

What area of your life do YOU need to process?

_____

_____

_____

_____

What undesirable experience from your past or present would you like to process in this area of your life?

_____

_____

_____

_____

_____

_____

_____

_____

How do you feel about what's going on in this area of your life?

Select between two and four current feelings in this area of your life from the feelings wheel.

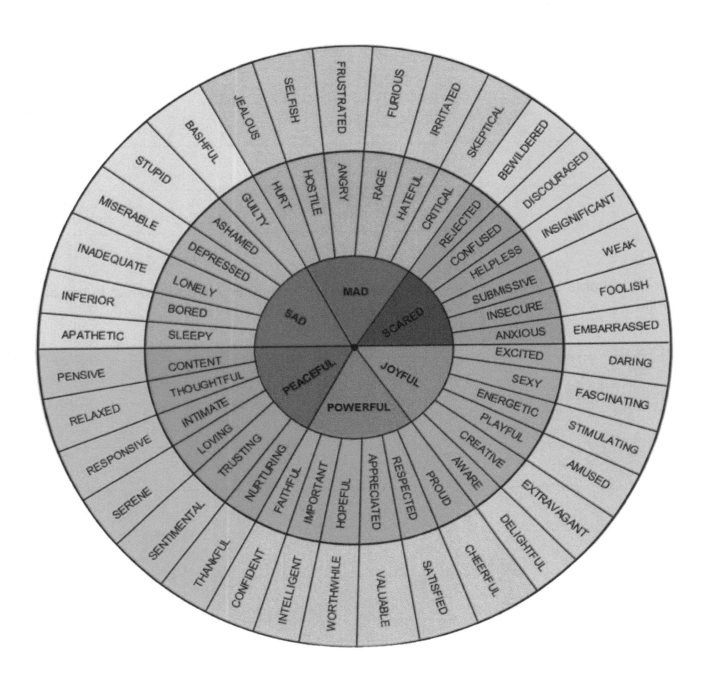

Feeling 1:

_____

Feeling 2:

_____

Feeling 3:

_____

Feeling 4:

_____

To take it a step further, think about how you would describe the feelings you've already named. Trust me, it will drive the point home even more in order to raise awareness. It will help you figure out what these feelings mean in the next step of your 4A Process inner conversation.

Here's a list of definitions for the feelings wheel I've made for you.

FEELINGS WHEEL DEFINITIONS

SAD

Word	Definition
Guilty	responsible for a specified wrongdoing; culpable.
Bashful	reluctant to draw attention to oneself; shy.
Ashamed	embarrassed or guilty because of one's actions, characteristics, or associations.
Stupid	lacking intelligence or common sense.
Depressed	(of a person) in a state of unhappiness and low morale; (of an economic market) characterized by a sustained fall in output and employment.
Miserable	wretchedly unhappy or uncomfortable; feeling or expressing extreme unhappiness or discomfort.
Lonely	sad because one has no friends or company.
Inadequate	lacking the quality or quantity required; insufficient for a purpose.
Bored	feeling weary and impatient because one is unoccupied or lacks interest in one's current activity.
Inferior	lower in rank, status, or quality.
Sleepy	feeling or showing a strong desire to sleep.
Apathetic	showing or feeling no interest, enthusiasm, or concern.

MAD

Word	Definition
Hurt	cause physical pain or injury to.
Jealous	feeling or showing envy of someone or their achievements and advantages.
Hostile	showing or feeling opposition or dislike; unfriendly.
Selfish	(of a person, action, or motive) lacking consideration for others; concerned chiefly with one's own personal profit or pleasure.
Angry	feeling or showing strong annoyance, displeasure, or hostility; full of anger.
Frustrated	feeling or expressing distress and annoyance, especially because of inability to change or achieve something.
Rage	violent, uncontrollable anger.
Furious	extremely angry; full of anger or energy; violent or unrestrained.
Hateful	arousing, deserving of, or filled with hatred.
Irritated	showing or feeling slight anger; annoyed.
Critical	expressing adverse or disapproving comments or judgments.
Skeptical	not easily convinced; having doubts or reservations.

SCARED

Word	Definition
Rejected	dismiss as inadequate, inappropriate, or not to one's taste.
Bewildered	perplexed and confused; very puzzled.
Confused	(of a person) unable to think clearly; bewildered.
Discouraged	having lost confidence or enthusiasm; disheartened.
Helpless	unable to defend oneself or to act without help.
Insignificant	too small or unimportant to be worth consideration.
Submissive	ready to conform to the authority or will of others; meekly obedient or passive.
Weak	lacking the power to perform physically demanding tasks; lacking strength or energy.
Insecure	not confident or assured; uncertain and anxious.
Foolish	lacking good sense or judgment; unwise.
Anxious	experiencing worry, unease, or nervousness, typically about an imminent event or something with an uncertain outcome.
Embarrassed	feeling or showing embarrassment; ashamed or humiliated.

PEACEFUL

Word	Definition
Content	in a state of peaceful happiness or satisfaction.
Pensive	engaged in, involving, or reflecting deep or serious thought.
Thoughtful	absorbed in or involving thought.
Relaxed	free from tension and anxiety; at ease.
Intimate	closely acquainted; familiar, close and personal.
Responsive	reacting quickly and positively; showing sensitivity.
Loving	feeling or showing love or great care.
Serene	calm, peaceful, and untroubled; tranquil.
Trusting	showing a belief that someone or something is reliable, good, honest, effective, etc.
Sentimental	prompted by feelings of tenderness, sadness, or nostalgia; appealing to the emotions, especially in an excessive way.
Nurturing	care for and encourage the growth or development of.
Thankful	pleased and relieved, expressing gratitude and relief.

POWERFUL

Word	Definition
Confident	feeling or showing confidence in oneself; self-assured
Faithful	loyal, constant, and steadfast; remaining true to someone or something
Intelligent	having or showing intelligence, especially of a high level
Important	of great significance or value; likely to have a profound effect on success, survival, or well-being
Worthwhile	worth the time, money, or effort spent; of value or importance
Hopeful	feeling or inspiring optimism about a future event
Valuable	worth a great deal of money or highly prized; useful or helpful
Appreciated	recognized the full worth of something or someone; welcomed and enjoyed
Satisfied	contented; pleased; fulfilled
Respected	admired by others for one's achievements, virtues, or personal qualities; accorded deference or esteem
Cheerful	noticeably happy and optimistic; giving a sense of comfort or well-being
Proud	feeling deep pleasure or satisfaction as a result of one's achievements, qualities, or possessions.

JOYFUL

Word	Definition
Aware	having knowledge or perception of a situation or fact
Delightful	causing delight; charming
Extravagant	lacking restraint in spending money or using resources
Creative	relating to or involving the imagination or original ideas
Amused	finding something funny or entertaining
Playful	fond of games and amusement; lighthearted
Stimulating	encouraging or arousing interest or enthusiasm
Energetic	possessing or involving great physical or mental energy
Fascinating	extremely interesting or attractive; charming
Sexy	sexually attractive or exciting
Daring	adventurous and unafraid; bold
Excitement	a feeling of great enthusiasm and eagerness

Address It

Unpack & Discover the Root of Your Feelings

After identifying the feelings you specifically have, labeling them, and defining them, it's time to move your inner conversation to the place called ADDRESS IT within the 4A Process.

Why is that?

I've noticed many people would stop at the place of being aware of what's going on within them because of two reasons.

1. They get a chance to vent their feelings and it makes them feel better.
2. They don't know what to do beyond knowing what they are feeling and just simply stop at being aware of what they are feeling.

"I'd rather go through the ugly part of processing my emotions than appear good on the outside but be ugly on the inside," I always say.

With that said, let us dive into the ugly in order to emerge internally beautiful on the other side.

Answer these questions below to begin to ADDRESS IT:

What's making you feel the emotions you identified in the Awareness step?

Insert feelings from the Awareness area into the blank spaces.

Feeling 1:

I feel _____ because…

_____

_____

_____

_____

_____

_____

Feeling 2:

I feel _____ because…

_____

_____

_____

_____

_____

Feeling 3:

I feel _____ because…

_____

_____

_____

_____

_____

Feeling 4:

I feel _____ because...

_____

_____

_____

_____

_____

What expectations did you have in this area of your life that were not satisfied, causing you to feel this way?

_____

_____

_____

_____

_____

_____

_____

Where do you think this expectation came from?

_____

_____

_____

_____

_____

_____

_____

_____

_____

_____

_____

_____

_____

_____

What are you afraid to see happen in this area of your life if these feelings continue?

_____

_____

_____

_____

_____

_____

_____

_____

_____

_____

_____

_____

_____

What is ultimately at the root of how you're feeling right now in this area of your life?

Accept It

To begin the process of change, be honest with yourself. Don't be ashamed.

I know it got a little ugly in the process of addressing your inner conversation and digging deeper into the root cause of your feelings. If you don't practice addressing your feelings, you may be feeling emotionally exhausted right now. You might also believe that all of your feelings are the result of someone else's actions and what they did to make you feel that way.

Perhaps not. Getting to the bottom of what you were feeling may have helped you see yourself more clearly, but these feelings remain unresolved even though "you got it."

Now that you've reached this point in your inner conversation, it's time to face the facts of your situation. It's time to accept responsibility in this situation.

OUCH!

I know some of you despise this word and believe you have no control over how you feel right now.

I respectfully disagree. You will not grow if you cannot take responsibility for why you are feeling this way, even if someone has wronged you. That is, you will not grow at all.

You would have wasted your time investigating your inner conversation if you couldn't accept it. Whatever "it" may be,

We all have a choice now in how we respond to something that is happening or has happened.

This is the point in your conversation where you will gain confidence, hope, clarity, and faith in your ability to change the situation by changing your inner conversation.

OK, enough of me trying to persuade you to accept responsibility.

Answer the following questions and see for yourself what happens.

What is the current reality of this area in my life?

_____

_____

_____

_____

_____

_____

_____

_____

_____

_____

_____

_____

_____

_____

What limiting beliefs have you accepted about yourself in this area of your life?

Here are some examples of some limiting beliefs people have in the 6 different areas of life:

Health and wellness:
"I'll never be able to lose weight."
"I don't have the motivation to exercise."
"I'm not good enough to take care of my mental health."
"I am too damaged or broken for spirituality to make a difference in my life."

Life fulfillment:
"I'm not creative enough to pursue my passions."
"I don't have enough time to do things that make me happy."
"I'm not deserving of living a fulfilling life."

Relationships:
"I'm not good at making friends."
"I'm afraid of being rejected in romantic relationships."
"I can't trust anyone in my family or professional relationships."

Personal productivity:
"I'm too disorganized to be productive."
"I'm not disciplined enough to stick to a schedule."
"I'm not capable of achieving my goals."

Career & Business:
"I'm not qualified for the job I want."
"I'll never be successful in my career."
"I'm not good enough to start my own business."

Finances:
"I'll always be in debt."
"I'm not good at managing my money."
"I don't deserve to have financial stability."

That was just an example.

So, let me ask you again: what limiting beliefs have you accepted about yourself in this area of your life?

_____

_____

_____

_____

_____

_____

_____

_____

_____

_____

_____

_____

What role are you playing in what's happening in this area of your life?

We all have a choice to make now in how we respond to something happening or what has happened.

_____

_____

_____

_____

_____

_____

_____

_____

_____

_____

_____

_____

What are some things you need to forgive yourself for right now about this situation?

Accelerate

I know that you've been on a journey that you may not have been on before when processing your inner conversation. You've become aware, addressed what you've become aware of, and accepted some aspects of yourself that you may not have been aware of. It's okay. It's normal to feel this way. That being said, you should be feeling emotionally drained and ready to stop processing and go relax your mind. I get it. In fact, most people try to skip right to this part of the process in their inner conversation and just come up with solutions.

The problem with that is that you come up with action steps and plans from an unhealed and anxious place in order to stop the undesirable feelings you begin to experience. In turn, you will probably start to use these actions as bandages instead of really getting to know yourself or getting the right internal surgery to heal.

It's time to move forward with faith to get rid of those feelings and end this inner conversation process with purpose, power, and precision.

It's time to accelerate forward!

Answer the following questions to begin accelerating.

Would you like to replace your old expectation of this situation with a new one? If so, what do you expect now?

_____

_____

_____

_____

_____

_____

How do you want to feel in this area of your life now?

It is imperative that you intentionally replace the feelings you have been experiencing in this area of your life with new feelings, by FAITH.

Select between 2 - 4 feelings from the feelings wheel and answer below

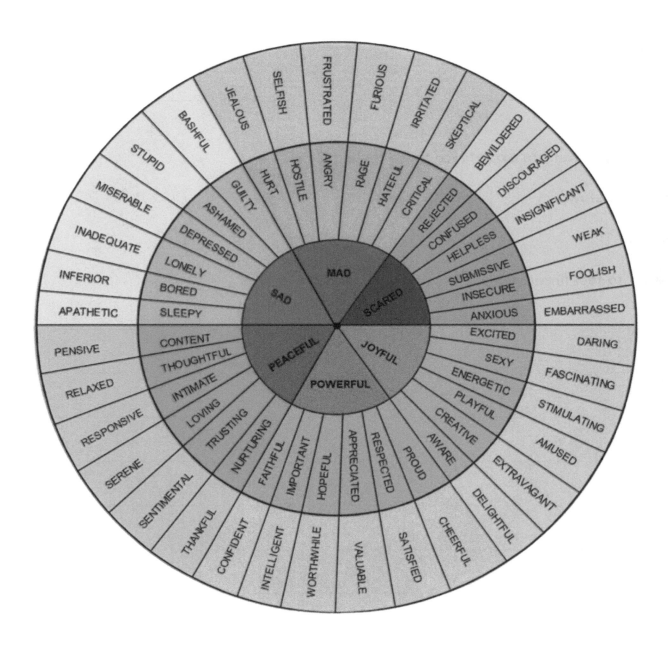

Feeling 1:

_____

Feeling 2:

_____

Feeling 3:

_____

Feeling 4:

_____

Why do you want to experience these feelings?

Answer below:

<u>Feeling 1:</u>

I want to feel *(insert feeling from feelings wheel)* **because...**

_____

_____

_____

_____

_____

Feeling 2:

I want to feel *(insert feeling from feelings wheel)* because…

_____

_____

_____

_____

_____

_____

Feeling 3:

I want to feel *(insert feeling from feelings wheel)* because…

_____

_____

_____

_____

_____

_____

Feeling 4:

I want to feel *(insert feeling from feelings wheel)* **because...**

_____

_____

_____

_____

_____

_____

What LIMITLESS beliefs do you choose to accept in this area of your life?

Your limitless beliefs are the opposite of the limiting beliefs you identified in the ACCEPT it part of the process.

It's very important to replace those beliefs in order to move forward in faith and in good emotional health.

Here are some limitless beliefs examples:

Health and Wellness:
"My body is capable of healing itself."
"I am worthy of self-care and self-love."
"I can create a healthy lifestyle that works for me."

Life Fulfillment:
"I am capable of achieving my goals and dreams."
"I have unique gifts and talents to share with the world."
"My creativity and recreation are essential to my well-being."

Relationships:
"I am deserving of healthy and fulfilling relationships."
"I am capable of giving and receiving love."
"I can set healthy boundaries in my relationships."

Personal Productivity:
"I am capable of managing my time effectively."
"I am capable of balancing my responsibilities and hobbies."
"I am constantly improving my productivity habits."

Career & Business:
"I have valuable skills and expertise to offer."
"I can achieve success and fulfillment in my career or business."
"My work can make a positive impact on others."

Finances:
"I am capable of creating abundance in my life."
"I am worthy of financial stability and security."
"I am developing healthy money management habits."

So again, What LIMITLESS beliefs do you choose to accept in this area of your life?

_____

_____

_____

_____

_____

_____

_____

_____

_____

_____

_____

_____

_____

_____

Action Steps Introduction:

Congratulations on reaching the home stretch of completing your 4A Process and moving forward to a healthy life and emotions. It is crucial to have the right mindset as you set your action steps to move forward. It's to identify action steps that align with your current healing journey.

Remember that you have just set a new expectation for what you want to see happen in your life. You have also identified what you want to feel now, as compared to what you were feeling before, and why you want to feel those emotions. But just thinking about your expectations and feelings is not enough. It is time to set worthwhile action steps to move forward towards the emotions, life, and relationships you desire.

Consider the following questions:

Who do you need to have a conversation with to begin moving towards your desired feelings? Why do you need to converse with them?

Is it to work through a conflict, learn something new, gain a clearer understanding, share openly and honestly about something, or just to have someone hold you accountable?

Having a conversation with someone can be a great way to support your personal growth and healing, especially after taking the time to reflect on your own thoughts and feelings.

Now, it's time to identify specific action steps that you can take. Think about what needs to be done to accomplish them and when they need to be completed. I love the completion part because without a set time, something is merely a dream or a desire, not a decision. Changes in life happen by making decisions, not by merely having desires. So, let's get started with the action steps.

ACTION STEPS
What actions are you going to take this week?

Action Step 1:

_____

_____

_____

_____

What needs to be done to accomplish this action step?

_____

_____

_____

_____

_____

_____

_____

_____

What date and time will this action step be completed by?

_____

_____

Action Step 2:

_____

_____

_____

_____

What needs to be done to accomplish this action step?

_____

_____

_____

_____

_____

_____

_____

_____

What date and time will this action step be completed by?

_____

_____

Action Step 3:

_____

_____

_____

_____

What needs to be done to accomplish this action step?

_____

_____

_____

_____

_____

_____

_____

What date and time will this action step be completed by?

_____

_____

Action Step 4:

_____

_____

_____

What needs to be done to accomplish this action step?

_____

_____

_____

_____

_____

_____

_____

_____

What date and time will this action step be completed by?

_____

_____

Action Step 5:

_____

_____

_____

_____

What needs to be done to accomplish this action step?

_____

_____

_____

_____

_____

_____

_____

_____

What date and time will this action step be completed by?

_____

_____

Conclusion

In conclusion, after going through the 4A Process, it is essential to prioritize self-care and avoid reverting to unhealthy coping mechanisms. This is a critical step in the journey of healing and maintaining a healthy inner conversation. Taking 30 minutes to 1 hour to do something relaxing and enjoyable is an excellent way to refill your spirit and soul. Engaging in healthy activities can help you avoid falling back into old patterns of behavior.

Some healthy outlet activities that you can engage in include:

- Going for a walk
- Engaging in a creative hobby
- Taking a break from thinking and performing
- Exercising
- Taking a nap
- Meditating
- Reading a book
- Listening to music
- Cooking or baking
- Gardening
- Journaling
- Spending time in nature
- Taking a relaxing bath
- Practicing mindfulness

It is important to find what works best for you. When doing these activities, try to do them in solitude, as it gives you time to let the process you have just completed soak in without the influences of other people.

Avoid social media, as it can fill your mind with distractions that can cloud your thoughts and feelings from the work you have just done. The goal is to find a way to refill yourself because you have just undergone soulful surgery. You are spiritually and soulistically vulnerable, so it is important to intentionally fill yourself back up with healthy activities.

As you continue to use this process, your brain will become rewired on how to handle your unhealthy inner conversations.

Embrace this habit of healing and continue to engage in a healthy inner conversation. This will lead to self-discovery, growth, and a more fulfilling life.

Welcome to the continual journey of self-care and inner peace.

Key Takeaways

Expectations are the internal voice that tells you what is right and wrong, and they are not always bad.

We must understand the role expectations play in order to comprehend the journey of our unhealthy internal conversations that lead to unhealthy actions and relationships.

Expectations get a bad reputation when they are not met, leading people to set lower or no expectations to avoid disappointment.

It's important to understand where expectations come from and what happens when they are not met to comprehend the journey of unhealthy internal conversations.

Evaluating our experiences is the best way to learn from them

The first step to dealing with unhealthy conversations with ourselves that arise from unmet expectations is becoming aware of what we are feeling.

Labeling our feelings can help us understand and process them more effectively.

Many people stop at the awareness stage because they either feel better just by venting or they don't know what to do beyond being aware of their feelings.

It's crucial to go through the process of addressing your emotions and not just stop at the surface level of awareness.

Processing your emotions may be difficult and uncomfortable, but it's better to go through the "ugly" in order to emerge as a healthier and more authentic version of yourself.

To make a change, start by being honest with yourself about how you feel and don't be ashamed.

After addressing your inner conversation, it's time to face the facts and accept responsibility.

Taking responsibility is crucial for personal growth, even if someone else has wronged you.

You have a choice in how you respond to a situation, and accepting responsibility gives you the power to change it.

Accepting responsibility brings confidence, hope, clarity, and faith in your ability to change the situation.

Processing your inner conversation can be emotionally draining but it's important to not skip steps.

Coming up with solutions from an unhealed and anxious place can lead to using bandages instead of true healing.

It's time to move forward with faith and end the inner conversation process with purpose, power, and precision.

About Author

Meet Darius Brown, author of "The Best Conversation You Ever Had Workbook" and your trusted Conversation Coach. With over 11 years of experience as a corporate trainer for sales in various companies across the United States, Darius has honed his expertise in effective communication and personal growth.

Darius's journey began in the corporate world, where he trained sales professionals on how to communicate effectively with clients and achieve sales targets. However, he soon realized that his true passion lay in helping people apply these communication skills to their personal lives. Darius started breaking down conversational principles and sales techniques in a way that his trainees could apply to their everyday interactions in response to the transformative power of meaningful conversations. The results were astonishing, with trainees reporting improved personal relationships, conflict resolution, and a deeper understanding of their loved ones.

Recognizing the impact of personal challenges on sales performance, Darius bridged the gap by incorporating inner conversations and personal growth into his training programs. By helping sales professionals navigate their inner challenges, he empowered them to cultivate a positive mindset, build resilience, and enhance their overall performance in sales conversations.

Darius's comprehensive coaching programs, developed as valuable employee benefits, have garnered acclaim from a diverse clientele, including famous celebrities, C-suite executives, and high-performing sales teams. However, his focus remains on putting the individual at the center of his work, guiding them through the 4A Process and REAP conversation method to unlock their full potential and create deeper, more fulfilling relationships both at work and at home.

As your Conversation Coach, Darius is dedicated to your personal transformation and the art of extraordinary conversations. His multiple books on having better conversations with yourself and others serve as invaluable resources for personal growth and connection. With Darius by your side, you can navigate your inner conversations, embrace personal growth, and cultivate authentic relationships that make a lasting impact.

Additional Resources

The Best Conversation You Ever Had With Yourself:
Embark on a transformative journey towards self-mastery with "The Best Conversation You Ever Had With Yourself." This book introduces the 4A Process, guiding you to master your inner conversation and unlock a new level of self-awareness, personal growth, and fulfillment. Discover the power of meaningful self-talk and unleash your true potential.

The Best Conversation You Ever Had:
"The Best Conversation You Ever Had" is your comprehensive resource for cultivating fruitful conversations and improving communication skills. This workbook builds upon the ideas in the acclaimed book, "The Best Conversation You've Ever Had with Yourself," giving you practical tools and techniques to approach conversations with intentionality. Explore the REAP Conversation Method: Rapport Building, Engaging Questions, Active Listening, and Proper Response Tools. Learn to create meaningful connections beyond small talk and foster understanding and growth. This workbook empowers you to become a master communicator, transforming your interactions into transformative moments. Get ready to navigate conversations with confidence, authenticity, and impact.

You Hired Them Now What?
Discover the ultimate guide to team building with "You Hired Them Now What?: 34 Conversation Activities To Build Rapport & Connection With Your New Team." Your Conversation Coach, Darius Brown presents 34 powerful activities to ignite motivation, enhance collaboration, and create a high-performing team.

Conversational Anxiety:
Take control of your conversations and overcome anxiety with "Conversational Anxiety." This book provides practical strategies and tools to help you navigate and conquer listening and sharing anxiety. Learn how to establish healthy boundaries, honor your own needs and emotions, and foster connections that feel freeing, connecting, vulnerable, and intentional.

These books, along with other valuable resources, can be found on our website at www.getyourconversationcoach.com/store

I believe in the power of continuous learning and personal growth, and these resources will support you in developing effective communication skills and navigating the complexities of conversations.

Visit my website today to explore these books and embark on a journey towards empowering and fulfilling conversations.

Feedback

Hey there! I hope you've enjoyed this workbook. I value your thoughts and opinions, and I would love to hear your feedback. If you have any suggestions, comments, or just want to say hi, feel free to reach out to me at darius@imdariusbrown.com.

Your feedback helps me make this workbook even better! Looking forward to hearing from you :)

www.imdariusbrown.com/store

Made in the USA
Columbia, SC
13 October 2023